RSCN. SRN.

and then —

'A Voyage of a Lifetime'

by

Brandy Thomas

First published in 2002 by
Brandy Thomas

Copyright © Brandy Thomas 2002

ISBN 0-9542148-0-3

Designed and produced by

The Short Run Book Company Limited
St Stephen's House
Arthur Road
Windsor
Berkshire SL4 1RY

For Peter (J.J)

For my family, Scott, Gill, Max and Olivia

Brandy, aged 17yrs,
at The Royal Hospital for Sick Children,
Glasgow

CHAPTER 1

By 1952 I had completed my Sick Childrens' training in a tough part of Glasgow, (near the Gorbals), at the Royal Hospital for Sick Children, Yorkhill, and on the 1st January 1953, having of course first celebrated Hogmanay, I travelled to London with my good friend Jean.

She too had just qualified, and Matron at St Thomas' Hospital had accepted us for further training, 'provided that we can understand you' she said! At that stage in our life, I have to admit that we did have a VERY broad Glaswegian accent, mainly so that we could talk to, and understand the children there!

Me with the sick children

For the past three years, we had worked tremendously hard, but although we understood that coming to the big city would mean even more hard grind, we were prepared to see it through in order to become State Registered nurses, and on the English register at that!

Jean's Mother, and our previous Matron, had both trained there, so of course we felt that we knew a little bit about the place.

The hospital was situated immediately opposite Big Ben, and the Houses of Parliament, so all the wards in the seven blocks looked out on to this wonderful panoramic view. We had no excuse for NOT knowing the correct time!

The men working on the tourists boats up and down the Thames, would enjoy shouting through their tanoids, that the seven blocks of the hospital were named after the seven days of the week, but of

*The Festival Hall taken from my room in Waterloo Bridge Hospital,
attached to St Thomas' Hospital, where I nursed in the Skin Ward.*

course this was absolute rubbish! Each ward was actually called
Charity, Elizabeth, City of London or George, Beatrice, Scutari or Mary
etc etc, and the sister in charge of each one was named accordingly.

Sunday lunch menu for the patients had to be taken round each bed
in the ward, by one of the junior nurses. Jean and I were having
trouble making ourselves understood, just as Matron had feared, so at
night, in the bath at the nurses home, we would practise the menu out
loud....Roast beef, Yorkshire pudding, and Horse Radish sauce, in
our most exaggerated English accent!! The other nurses found this
hilarious! Today we both have very normal accents, but with a slight
hint of our past coming through, especially on the telephone, we are told.

Working hard did not stop us from playing hard however, as there
was so much to see and do in London. Many times we suffered from
lack of sleep, but it was more than worth it! One occasion was the all
night ball at the Royal Festival Hall. I can still remember eating those
bacon and eggs there at 5 a.m. and then reporting on duty at 7.30 a.m!

Our salary was very low, but occasionally we were given free
tickets for the cinema, or the theatre, and as long as we wore our
outdoor uniform, we also had free passes on the buses and tubes.

Me as Charge Nurse in Elizabeth, wearing the distinctive lace cap and Nightingale badge

If the tickets were for Sadlers Wells, or Covent Garden, we would dress up to the nines, in order to impress at the ticket office, and therefore given the best seats, even though they knew we were nurses!

Boyfriends were in abundance, either being the brothers of fellow nurses, or more usually medical students, or fully qualified doctors, who had not gotten around to marrying!

My special friend, however, to whom I had been introduced by a former patient, was a Senior Detective Superintendent. He was involved in the problems of high powered crime in Room 109 of the C.I.D. at Scotland Yard! His work frequently entailed visiting the underworld in the pubs down the East End of London.

To enable him to give the aura of normality, he liked to take someone like me with him, to talk to the other customers. He would ring me at the nurses home, and say that he was coming in a taxi...that the driver was another plain clothed detective, and under the seat a tape recorder was running!

On reaching our destination, complete with peak cap and jeans, we would set off to meet

Det. Superintendent Peter Vibart

My only photo of Jean

some shady character, who was hopefully awaiting his backhander, in exchange for parting with some vital information! I was asked to look like a policewoman, which was not too difficult, being 5' 7½" tall! I am not certain if I actually heard the end of that particular story, but I do remember having a splendid evening out afterwards, at the Pigalle Club, in Piccadilly, and many months later hearing that the infamous jewel thief Padola, had been caught. The praise in all the National Newspapers was being attributed to Detective Superintendent Peter Vibart!

One very exciting outing springs to mind. The two detectives were on duty at Ascot for the day, and were able to take two of us as guests into the Paddock, where we enjoyed mixing with the rich and famous, AND the bizarre! We had a few bets on the horses, but I don't recall either of us winning any money! We stopped off at The Pantiles, at Bagshot, on the way home for a swim and a meal.

Three years flashed, past, and the fourth year I spent very happily as a Charge nurse in a Womens Surgical Ward, where we had thirty patients. It was considered a great honour to be asked by a ward sister to become her charge nurse for a year, and I was thrilled when Sister Elizabeth approached me.

Her name was Miss Gwynneth Rowe, one of the old school of nurses, strict, but honest, and a great sense of humour into the bargain. The junior nurses enjoyed it there, and learnt a great deal, and I was proud to hold the fort on Miss Rowe's off duty hours, weekends and holidays.

Just as I was beginning to wonder what next to do with my life, an Australian Doctor, who was acting locum on my ward, remarked that I was the type of girl who would love his country. I laughed saying, chance would be a fine thing, and how did he imagine that I could earn enough here as a nurse, to venture to the other side of the world!

The very next day came the reply....His Father-in-Law Mr Buckley, was Agent General of New South Wales House in the Strand, in London, and he was apparently interested in meeting me with a view to a position on a ship, offering a free first class RETURN passage to Oz!! It seemed too good to be true!

CHAPTER 2

On the following day, my off duty hours happened to be in the morning from 10 a.m.-1 p.m.

Without hesitation, I dashed up to the Strand, and by 10.45 I was standing outside Mr Buckley's office.

I found myself rehearsing who I was, and why I had come, etc, but I need not have worried. He welcomed me with open arms! His son-in-law Dr Doug Tracy had explained my position to him fully. He knew my name, my qualifications, and even, it seemed, my personality!

The first job offered to me was to escort an elderly gentleman with Diabetes. The only treatment, all being well, would be Insulin injections, discreetly scrutinizing his diet, and ensuring that he did not drink too much of the dreaded alcohol on board!

The date of this journey was just a few weeks before my year's contract was up as a Charge nurse in Elizabeth ward.

Never mind, I thought, Matron would arrange something to let me be released in time....but I was wrong!!! 'You are under contract for a whole year nurse' she said, 'and a year it must be'. What a blow!!

As you can imagine I was devastated! Why on earth had fate dealt me such a cruel blow? That sort of chance could surely come but only once in a lifetime.

I was reminded in no uncertain terms that 'a contract is NOT drawn up to be broken'. I thought entirely the opposite at that moment!!

Total depression set in for a few days, but Christmas was approaching and there was a great deal of preparation to be done on the ward.

Our theme for that year was 'The Girls of St Trinians', so masses of dressing up clothes to organise!

Giles, the Express newspaper cartoonist, had kindly given Sister some original drawings to hang above each bed, which gave the whole thing a professional look.

*Elizabeth Ward, St. Thomas' Hospital, dressed overall
as The Girls of St. Trinians, with original Giles cartoons over each bed.*

Relations of patients always gave us great support on these occasions, spending most of Christmas Day with us, and the poor unfortunates who had no choice but to stay in hospital over the festive season.

27th December 1956 Mr Buckley wished to see me again! (Strangely the 27th December was the date my son was born 7 years later!) This time the date would be OK and was a completely different job, with just a *single* first class passage. As if I would mind!

I must say I was very proud to have completed my year's contract, as a Charge nurse, in Florence Nightingale's Hospital, but I couldn't wait to find out what sort of task I was going to be asked to do for four weeks on a first class ship to Australia!

Not only did it involve accompanying an eleven month old illegitimate baby to Melbourne, but I would be responsible for keeping an eye on the Mother, who would be secretly travelling on the same ship, but on a different deck! WOW!

The paid first class passage for me would be one way only this time, but I could work as a nurse to save my return fare, as nurses pay in Australia was known to be extremely good.

I would also be responsible for keeping the secret from all other passengers for the entire four week trip, the only concession being that, about four or five of the crew members would also know the truth. This was essential for Customs purposes alone.

I badly needed some new bikinis, and clothes for this trip, so spent the next few days, scouring the London boutiques and large stores, having a whale of a time!

CHAPTER 3

I staggered back to the nurses home, my head buzzing with excitement. The date would be o.k. this time thank goodness, but I must give the whole thing a great deal of thought.

With whom could I discuss such a secret journey?

What was the mother like I wondered? I must meet her as soon as possible. Where is she, and why on earth does she want to do such a thing?

I had been told that she was a Catholic, and able to receive all the help she requires from the Catholic Family Bureau in London. She did not mind me being a member of the Church of Scotland.

She had apparently run away from home in Melbourne, in order to have, and, as she thought, to hide, her illegitimate baby, in England. What she did not know however, was that the little boy must go back to Australia before his first birthday. That is the law.

My three years training at the Royal Hospital for Sick Children in Glasgow, at such an early age, had given me a rare insight into children and their parents, but never had I come across such a strange story before. Luckily, I always seemed to stand up to any challenge thrown at me in life, and luckily this was to be no exception! At nineteen, I had found myself in charge of an operating theatre in Glasgow because Sister had gone off sick.

Surgeons are notoriously short tempered, especially with the unscrubbed junior nurses unfortunately, who are desperately doing their best to please everyone at the same time, under very difficult circumstances. However I must say these men treated me with great respect, probably to keep me calm, and I learnt a huge amount from them all.

One young nurse dropped the entire tray of sterilized instruments on the floor, which could have been disastrous. These days they would be autoclaved and disposable, after only one use.

My friend Jean and I were often on call at night, in Glasgow, having worked all day of course. Our bleeper would go off, perhaps in the middle of washing our hair, so the turban was quickly tied round the head, the wrap around overall flung over our cotton pants and bra', and down we would go to set up the theatre, having been told whether it was for an emergency appendix, an obstruction, or even a fractured skull!

Weekends on the wards in a Childrens Hospital were sometimes a nightmare, especially on a Sunday. There were virtually no porters on general duties, so if we were unfortunate enough to have the death of a baby or child, it was the nurses responsibility to carry the tiny white shrouded corpse to the top floor of the hospital during the night.

The lift reached the floor below this, so one was obliged to climb the last flight of steps on foot, the shadow on the tiled wall in front of you, portraying the body of the child stretched out on either side of your own body. Not a pretty sight, and something I shall never forget in a hurry!

The old tramcar was still in use while I worked in Glasgow, and my stint in casualty was hectic! Children used to play 'dare' across the tram lines, would you believe, so we had more than one amputation! Parents would come rushing in,clutching a child, and shouting hysterically, 'ma wain's fa'en aff a dyke'. This roughly translated meant that he or she had fallen off a wall (usually a very high wall!).

Night duty Casualty in London was yet another story, but we had some hilarious moments as well .... The tramps used to come in at night to have their feet soaked in Permaganate of Potash, and of course to find some warmth, and a welcome cup of tea!

In those days at least, we were not troubled with the drug problem,and there was very little violence towards the staff. The odd International football match would sometimes cause a stir in Casualty, when the rival fans arrived after a fisty cuffs, and a few drinks too many, continuing the brawl, in and out of the curtained cubicles!

Our greatest sadness was to see a young motor cyclist, who was completely disfiguered after smashing into a wall, or the odd model, ruined for life by a devastating car crash!

There was an unwritten rule in a London teaching hospital, to never say that it was too quiet in casualty. If you did, the world then seemed to go mad, the ambulances started arriving with sirens wailing, and there was mayhem for the rest of the night!

One thing used to bother me, and that was having treated a patient in casualty, and then helped the porter to wheel the stretcher to a ward, I would then be too busy to enquire after the patient, and follow their progress in the forthcoming weeks. Such a pity.

Sister Casualty was a tyrant...in fact I don't know how she got away with it, but she did, and the place was spotless and run like clockwork.

Now back to the baby....

No way can the child be adopted in this country legally, but the child would certainly be given excellent care and attention here at birth, either in a private clinic, or in a National Health Hospital.

The Mother's name was Kathleen, and the baby John Joseph was eleven months old, and living with foster parents down in Surrey.

The poor girl was of a very nervous disposition, unable to cope with everyday issues, let alone look after a baby for four weeks on board ship, which, although her own, she had never obviously ever handled. The thought too, of perhaps meeting other fellow travellers who might just know her family in Melbourne, the latter having no inkling of the truth at this point, and some of her brothers apparently being well known Australian Rules footballers.

She visualised her parents meeting her at the quayside, as the ship docked. No way could she handle the explanation which would be required if she arrived clutching a baby, and all the necessary accoutrements in tow. She wanted to tell them in her own time, in the future, in the safety of her own home. Also at this point she was certain that she did not want to keep the child anyway, feeling sure that her family would not accept the situation. The fact still remained ... she was absolutely responsible for arranging a safe passage, and escort,(me), for this baby to return to Australia before its very first birthday.

With all the very sick children I had nursed in the past, I could not believe that any mother could possibly think this way about her own child, especially such a gem as John Joseph... a healthy, bouncing, eleven month old, with a magnificent smile!

CHAPTER 4

My immediate problems were these....

Where should I go to meet the Mother secretly? Certainly not in her own flat I thought. Walls have ears!

This was speedily arranged by the Agent General himself, and we met in a pub.

How to contact the baby? Meet the Mother first I think.

Horrors! For customs purposes the child's name had to be stamped on MY passport!

With which two friends could I safely discuss this whole affair? I would have to practise a story which I could adhere to on board at all times.

The majority of the passengers would at some point wish to speak to me and the baby, especially when they realised I was only the nurse, and 'that he was going to his grandparents in Australia, because his parents had been killed in a car crash in England!!!

A ship of this size was a little like a very large village, where everyone seems to know everyone else's business, especially after four whole weeks!

THE MOTHER WAS TO TRAVEL SECRETLY ON BOARD THE SAME SHIP BUT ON A DIFFERENT DECK!!!

At our first meeting, Kathleen and I seemed to take to each other quite well, although we were as different as chalk to cheese. She was older than me I guessed. There was I, tall, strong and very healthy, hoping against hope that I was going to be able to tackle this whole business. There was she, small , timid and shy, very quietly spoken, and very highly strung!

The poor girl certainly needed help. She was shaking like a leaf, and her hands were trembling. She spoke with a soft 'Irish' accent, and very little 'g'day sport'.

Slowly but surely, I extracted the necessary immediate information which I required from her. She gave me an address in New Malden,

Surrey, where, she explained, I would find little Johnny in the very capable hands of a foster mother.

She confirmed that my single passage was booked and paid for, first class, together with the baby. He and I were to travel in style, in a cabin on 'E' deck. Luckily I had no worries of becoming homesick, having been away from home since my seventeenth birthday!

I returned to the nurses home once again, clutching the precious address, realizing that I had no telephone number for either the foster parents, or the real mother in an emergency!

One thing seemed clear...I was absolutely convinced that the Mother would be my major problem on board this ship!

Next day I travelled to New Malden in Surrey to see my protégé. That was a simply wonderful moment, as I had not tried previously to visualise, or imagine what the child would look like. In fact, Kathleen, unlike most mothers, had not described him to me at all, so I was absolutely thrilled to see before me such a really beautiful child, smiling and gurgling with delight at all the other children in the room.

He was nearly eleven months old, crawling everywhere, spotlessly dressed, with not a care in the world, and yet within the next two weeks, his little life was to be turned upside down.

There was I, twenty four years old, used to nursing very sick children, and now miraculously, I had been presented with this very healthy bouncing boy, to escort half way round the world, on my own!

Four weeks away lay his unknown fate. I would be compelled to leave him there, whatever the circumstances, to continue my journey on S.S.Orion, to my final destination in Sydney, and to my own relations, who were planning to meet me on board.

HE SMILED A MOST PERFECT SMILE...

CHAPTER 5

My next task seemed Herculean at first... I had to leave St Thomas' with all my gear which I had managed to accrue over the last four years, collect the baby from New Malden, with all the clothes, nappies, (no disposables in those days), pram etc etc, spend one night at a friend's flat in St John's Wood, (with the baby), and then find my way to the docks at Tilbury the next day!

I must say I had qualms over having an unknown baby's name written on my passport, but there was no going back. It just had to be done. The main purpose of this was so that each time we were grouped into sections at Customs on board, and at different ports of call, little Johnny could stay with me under 'E' (my maiden name being Eastwood). His surname began with the letter 'M' which would have necessitated my queuing up twice. We should also have been in the same queue as his Mother !

For many years after returning to the U.K. on my own, I still had the baby's name on my passport, and nothing would persuade my newer friends that I had not had an illegitimate child!!

Meantime, my parents had moved from Scotland to Hampshire, enabling me to leave much of my belongings with them, thank goodness. It also gave me the opportunity to spend a few days with them, say the fond farewells, and promise that I would come home one day. They had not seen too much of me while I was nursing in London, although I did fly home via British Caledonia sometimes. When in Glasgow, I would dash home for the day by train, but always needed to catch up on the sleep I had lost, whether on day or night duty at the time!

For many days my two friends bombarded me with questions to see if I had 'my story' fool proof for the inquisitive travellers on board.

Why was I taking the baby to Australia?

Where were the parents? Who was meeting me in Melbourne?

What was his surname, and has he any brothers and sisters?

Was I really just a nurse?

All these questions which would definitely be asked on this ship, and my reply had to be the same at all times...

His parents had been killed in a car crash in England, and I was taking him to his grandparents. No, I could not tell you where they live, or his surname, or if he has any brothers or sisters.

There was one question that I had not bargained on, and that was from two childless couples, who desperately wanted to adopt this gorgeous boy at the end of the journey. Could I arrange for them to speak to the grandparents at the quayside???

Everyone was sad to hear this heart-rending story of course, but Kathleen, watching from afar, must have been torn to shreds.

My dear friend Peter was absolutely intrigued by the whole idea, and being a detective, he tried to catch me out with my story. Why didn't the grandparents come to London for the child? Was the baby in the car when the parents were killed?

All I could think was, that, thank God, John Joseph was too young to remember all this, or to be able to correct me, and accuse me of telling huge porkies!!

The final evening came in the flat at St John's Wood. There we were, two girl friends, Peter, and a medical student friend called Pete Murray, whom I had known for several years, and this miraculous baby, still smiling as though he had known us all his little mixed up life! We had even borrowed a very smart cot for his one night, in which he slept soundly.

My trunk was packed,and in the hallway. Tears were flowing quietly, as we adults said our last goodbyes to each other. Even the one Scotch which I would normally enjoy, seemed wrong under the circumstances.

Peter, as usual, was going to be my last tower of strength, as he was driving us to the docks at Tilbury in the morning.

There was no noise or frivolity that evening. We were all eventually just staring at this fantastically good looking child, clutching his cuddly teddy bear. No one dared to speak in more than a whisper, in case we disturbed him.

Nothing I had experienced during my seven years nursing could be compared with this!

I was saying farewell to some of my dearest friends, and venturing into the unknown, with a colossal responsibility on my shoulders! (Little did I know then, that it would be the very last time I would ever see Peter, the Detective Superintendent..... Some years on , back in

England, I read that he had died, the force praising him for catching Podola, the jewel thief who shot dead a policeman, and some of the Great Train Robbers!)

The Flying Squad, his present wife, and I were the losers.

In my final year at St Thomas, another nurse and I were whizzing round London on a Vespa, in our off duty hours.

We accepted a bet from other nurses that we could not ride to Venice and back, during our two week holiday break.

The challenge was too great! We packed our panniers, and off we drove. That of course is another story, but right at this point I was grateful for all the experience it had given me, and didn't feel at all nervous or out of my depth, at the daunting prospects ahead.

1st February 1957, bright and early, dear little Johnny and I were driven down to the docks by Peter .... lock, stock and push chair!

We cautiously stepped onto the S.S.Orion. 1st class. Boomerang Excursion, Orient Line.

The sun was shining as if wishing us bon voyage!

The place was seething with passengers saying goodbye to loved ones, and the crew were everywhere, welcoming us aboard, and supervising the cranes, humping our trunks into the hold.

The ship was 'dressed overall' with ribbons and flags, and the streamers reached from the ship to the quay and back again, as the final link between friends before it sails. A truly moving moment.

S.S. Orion, in 1935 at Tilbury Docks.

CHAPTER 6

Suddenly, after all the excitement and dash of the last few weeks, I found myself alone with John Joseph, surrounded by masses of flowers from well wishers, in London and the Home Counties.

We were in a 1st class cabin on 'E' deck, complete with cot bolted to the wall on one side, and a portable fold up chair on the other side, next to the porthole. Even the potty was there!

This darling child, nearly eleven months old, and after all he had gone through in the last forty eight hours, was still smiling, making me sure that we were going to have a wonderful month together, whatever the complications.

J.J. and Brandy on S.S. Orion

Where in the ship was his Mother I wondered, but that I could find out all in good time. Perhaps she had changed her mind, run away, and not on the ship at all!!

Would this really remain a secret until we reached Melbourne. At least I knew she had paid for my 1stclass passage, one way, and I was clutching my passport, with the baby's name safely written inside. So, Australia here we come!!

It was decided in the ship's office in Piccadilly that a certain number of crew members would have to know about the circumstances of the mother and baby on board, especially as the mother was known to be irrational at times, and very

21

S.S. Orion at Tilbury Docks 1957

highly strung. Anything could happen (and did) in the next four weeks!

The final decision was to be made by the Captain. He had obviously had a meeting with some of his more senior officers before we sailed, and then I was informed of the select group... The Ship's Doctor, the 1ST officer, The Purser, and Colin, the children's chief dining room steward. They were sworn to secrecy....

Luckily I think everyone was taking the whole thing very seriously, knowing that Kathleen had threatened to jump overboard if any passenger found out about her secret.

The sea was calm that first evening, and Johnny slept, but I chose to have my evening meal brought to my cabin in order to keep an eye on him, half wondering, if perhaps, Kathleen might try to find out his whereabouts.

Earlier, I had managed to find my way to the Children's dining room, where John had literally gulped down his soup, and thoroughly enjoyed a plate of scrambled egg, followed by jelly and ice cream. I had decided to order something simple for his first meal, just in case he was inclined to seasickness.

Everyone was very helpful, and of course Colin introduced himself to me right away. He was young and good looking, and obviously had a way with young children.

The next morning I was brought tea in my bunk, and Johnny had some fruit juice. Breakfast for the children was at 7.45 a.m. Adults, any time from 8.15 a.m. in a separate dining room, whilst the children were very carefully looked after by some nannies in a playroom nearby. They seemed to have every facility to keep them amused, and I certainly felt that I could have my meal without worrying.

By early evening the ship began to roll a little, and much to my surprise, it was me who began to feel seasick! Johnny was o.k. luckily, but by next morning, having given him part of his porridge, I was forced to leave him in the capable arms of Colin, whilst I rushed off to the rail on 'B' deck!!

How embarrassing I thought, especially so early in the voyage, but Colin assured me that most adults had retired to their bunks by then! Apparently it is not unusual during the first few days of any cruise to be seasick whilst finding your 'sea legs' so

*Colin,
the Childrens' Dining Room steward*

to speak. The real test comes when you reach the Bay of Biscay, or some such other part of the journey.

Two days at sea, and I was beginning to observe my surroundings, and the other passengers, although still pleased to have an afternoon siesta with Johnny. I believe others, young and old, were doing the same!

By the fourth day people were beginning to ask me questions as predicted, but so far nothing that I couldn't handle.

The weather was absolutely lovely, so strolling round the deck with John in his pushchair was a great delight, and there were plenty of helping hands when I wished to go for a swim in the pool.

Even more fun was seeing Johnny crawling along the deck, with me in close pursuit, and then pulling himself up behind someone's chair, where they were playing cards or some board game, completely stopping the game in its tracks, and he becoming the centre of attraction as usual. No one seemed able to resist him!

In the childrens' creche, even though there were so many other lovely children around, he still appeared to steal the limelight, mainly I think, because people were beginning to talk about 'his tragedy'.

I knew Colin was in on the secret, but I was absolutely positive that it was better not to discuss the subject with him. Obviously I was in close contact with him at least three times a day, in the childrens' dining room.

The following day we would be arriving in Las Palmas in the Canary Islands.

J.J. and Brandy

*J.J. pulling himself up
behind people playing cards*

CHAPTER 7

I caught my first glimpse of Kathleen at breakfast time. She was sitting at a nearby table, looking her usual nervous self, but very attractive nevertheless, daintily dressed, and with her auburn hair framing a rather pale looking, but pretty face.

She was talking to some fellow travellers, no doubt discussing the experiences of their trip to Europe, and no doubt now looking forward to going home to friends and family. Little did they suspect the experience she had had, or the trauma of this journey home for her!

More and more passengers waylaid me on deck, or on the way to meals, wishing to know if I was really a trained nurse from St Thomas' Hospital in London, and had the baby's parents really been killed in a car crash in England?

One thing was very clear to me, it was no use Kathleen and I trying to ignore each other. That would make people even more suspicious in the long run. We could become friends on board, she could accompany me on trips ashore, and eventually even visit the baby in his bath, or look after him for me occasionally in the afternoons, to give me a break.

The two couples who persisted in their efforts to adopt J.J. asked me if the grandparents would be meeting me when we docked in Melbourne. That was sure a tricky question, because they would be meeting the ship to greet their daughter, but certainly not to be presented with either a nanny, or a grandchild, let alone four strangers wanting to adopt him!!

I decided to rely on the fact that when we did arrive, everyone, without exception, would be preoccupied with their own disembarking arrangements, and meeting friends and family, whereas I had arranged for a Priest to come straight to our cabin..... Johnny and I would NOT be around to be seen by anyone at that point!

Kathleen and J.J. in Capetown

On the 5th February,we stopped off at Las Palmas, in the Canary Islands. The weather was gorgeous. We reached the harbour by launch, and set off to see the sights in a pony and trap, but just after leaving the Hotel Santa Catalina, it unfortunately capsized, so the rest of the day was spent on foot!

Back on board in the evening, we had a dance which I was able to enjoy, safe in the knowledge that, not only was Johnny sound asleep, but that there was a night steward right outside his cabin door, listening to any murmur from he, or any of the other children, asleep in that area. The tannoy system called us if we were required. I also popped down from time to time.

The very next evening was the Captain's own cocktail party, which is always one of the highlights on any voyage by ship, but it was incredibly hot, and none of the children were feeling too well. John was unable to eat, he was developing a sweat rash, and by the evening there was no possibility that he would settle.

The stewards were always full of bright ideas, with all their experience, so they suggested taking his cot out into the corridor. Of course he was completely

Kathleen alone on the Orion

27

spoilt out there, almost becoming the ship's mascot, and because his gums were so inflamed, the chief steward gave him a huge turkey bone, scrubbed and scraped, to comfort him!

It was not unusual after this to find me pushing John round and round the deck, in the middle of the night, in my dressing gown, stopping to talk to the night watchman, or an officer having a breather.

Very soon though Johnny was his old self again, and generally he was not troubled by the heat.

The childrens' fancy dress party was enormously successful. There were powder puffs, sculptures and models, snowmen, peas in the pod etc. and of course John, as the Cow and Gate baby, complete with crown! Tea afterwards included ice cream teddy bears, and giant trifles.

Kathleen must have enjoyed the party, because in the evening she braced herself to come along and visit John Joseph in his bath. He thought of her as just another of his many 'aunties'.

She certainly could not be described as a chatterbox, but I did feel that she was at ease that evening, in the confines of the locked bathroom.

The only outright question she threw at me was to confirm that no passenger knew her secret?

I realised that neither of us could have a serious boyfriend on board, or for that matter too much to drink, but although we both had a flirt, and lots of fun, we did not get involved. (I met my husband to be on the RETURN JOURNEY between Sydney and Singapore, but that again is another story!)

The following evening, a 'Race' meeting was arranged. This took the form of wooden horses, which we wound up, to move very fast along an indoor track. Unbeknown to me, a lovely Irish chap called Derry, placed a huge bet on me to win, and I did, so the entire night turned into yet another great party, with champagne and beer flowing, even though it was very very windy on deck, and my bouffant style short evening dress, with a hoop under the skirt, just wouldn't stay down!!!

On Saturday 16th February, we were told that we would be spending the whole day in Capetown, South Africa, so Kathleen and I decided to take Johnny for a picnic in the park nearby, where we were able to show him the aviary, squirrels, and water lilies etc. It was very

More than one couple …

hot. I took a photograph of Kathleen and Johnny, with Table Mountain in the background.

In the afternoon, I had a built in baby sitter,(Kathleen), so I was able to accompany Colin, the childrens' steward, to the most beautiful swimming pool at Sea Point. Afterwards we had tea, and then back to the ship by taxi.(Nobody has ever known this until now, but because I wore my bikini to go in, I had forgotten to take my knickers

to come back in !) Thank goodness for the taxi!! The ship sailed at 11.30p.m

Sunday next day. A service in the lounge in the morning, and a jolly good sleep had by Johnny and I in the afternoon.

Somehow it all seemed too good to be true. Things were running too smoothly. Something had to give. Even a game of quoits on deck, being carefully scrutinized by some off duty officers, seemed a little weird, with the Mother and I playing on opposite sides of the net, and Johnny looking on, in the arms of one of his many admirers.

…. wanted to adopt J.J.

ALL THIS WAS ABOUT TO CHANGE...

CHAPTER 8

Having a whole day in the shadow of Table Mountain had been a real bonus for all of us, but the real reason was that the Suez Canal had been closed due to fighting, and we were forced to take the long route round. It also gave the crew a relaxing day off, and, I suspect, mainly due to the heat, many of them had rather too much to drink.

Colin, as I had previously mentioned, spent the afternoon with me at the pool, but I knew that he had the rest of the night off. We definitely did not discuss either the Mother or the baby, but he did know that Kathleen had offered to baby-sit for me, just for that afternoon.

Apparently he joined a few of his fellow crew members that evening, and during the course of their conversation, first talked about my going to the pool with him, and then blurted out to one and all, that Kathleen WAS the REAL Mother of the baby!!

Next morning the assistant purser came to see me, and to quietly explain the situation.

I was horrified of course, realising that one breath of this to Kathleen would mean a possible suicide attempt on her part!

The Purser, John Watkins, apparently had very strong words with Colin, and all other members who had been at the crew's makeshift party, were given a very serious warning that if this leaked out, there would be someone sacked immediately!

The following evening, we all enjoyed what was called 'The Seven Stars Club Dance', in the restaurant. I noticed Kathleen was sitting quietly on her own in a corner, but of course there was nothing unusual about that, as this was the pattern most of the time.

I think people generally were finding Kathleen hard going now, conversation stilted, and in the end, they gave up trying to socialise with her, because, after all, most of the passengers were understandably looking for a good time.

After the dance, a few of us retired to the second engineer's cabin to listen to records. I was again asked to confirm that Kathleen was the mother, so realised, at that moment, that the bush telegraph had been working overtime, and that the truth was out!

However, I decided to stick to my story, denying all round that this was the case. 'Don't be absurd, I said, how could she possibly be?'

The adult fancy dress dance was next on the agenda. I went as The Cruel Sea', obtaining green dye from the chef for my makeup, to make me look, well and truly seasick!

There were some brilliant ideas as usual. A honeymoon salad,(lettuce alone), Macbeth, Indian Rope trick, and Dwarf Man. One comedian called Dick was hauled up a rope for the snake charmers!

Johnny was almost walking by now, and 'talking' quite a lot. Such a wonderful child, and always laughing.

I met one poor chap called Jim, a Doctor, who was on his way to work at the gold mines in Kalgoorlie, but his wife on board, who was pregnant, had spent the entire trip down in her bunk!

Weather was deteriorating a little now, but I noticed Kathleen managing to keep on her feet sufficiently to do well in the deck tennis.

By the 23rd February, the ship really began to rock and roll! There were reports of passengers falling out of their bunks, and my tray capsized into my bed this morning! Thank goodness this time, however, I wasn't seasick! Johnny was finding the whole thing very funny!

Divine Service was cancelled next day with the storm increasing, and everyone finding it difficult to walk in a straight line.

My morning tea again slid into the bed, this time soaking the mattress. All deck games were now cancelled. Our tables in the dining room now had four wooden sides to them, to stop the crockery from sliding off, and the gangways had ropes!!!

Johnny and I played in the nursery all afternoon, and he is now able to hold the spoon and feed himself quite easily.

One morning I could see Kathleen, again sitting on her own, but near me in a deck chair. She was endeavouring to hear my conversation with one of the couples who were hoping to adopt Johnny. I could see her visibly going down hill!

The nearer our approach to Australia, the worse she became. I was much more alert to her movements, still feeling that I was very very responsible for her welfare.

Suddenly, with no warning, the inevitable happened... She had taken an overdose and tried to jump overboard.

Luckily for all of us, I arrived on the scene just in time, and from then on she was in the capable hands of the medics. It was a cry for help, I am sure, hoping desperately that I would be able to save her.

I felt a heavy load lifting off my young shoulders, and was then able to concentrate fully on my baby minding. The heat was intense. J.J's cot was in the corridor, and I still walked the decks with him at night!

Three and a half weeks had flown by, and as far as I was concerned the secret was still intact, even though I knew only too well that masses of rumours were being bandied about.

What else could be expected on a ship of this size? The passengers were all beginning to get a little bored of their surroundings, and not a little restless. As we all know you can have too much of a good thing sometimes.

Next stop was Freemantle, in Perth. We were up at 6a.m. and by 9a.m. I had taken J.J. ashore in a pushchair.

Perth's beaches and scenery are lovely, but I was not overly impressed by the town... We stopped for a few milk shakes, a new watch strap, and strapless bra' for me!!

Later that evening on board, I remember watching the film 'Red Shoes' with Moira Shearer, who originated from my hometown in Scotland.

The ship sailed very late that night, due to problems with a damaged lifeboat.

CHAPTER 9

Our personal letters appeared miraculously, and regularly from the Purser's office, so I was not surprised to hear that Kathleen had heard from the Catholic Welfare Bureau, in Melbourne. She was able to assure me that I would be met on board S.S. Orion by the Reverend Father Perkins, from East Melbourne.

I realised that it would be more like 10 p.m. when we docked, so asked her to be sure to let him know, that I would not allow the baby to travel anywhere that night.

Kathleen seemed nervous, but still not wishing to keep the baby to show to her parents. She was relying on me to arrange for the safe delivery of poor little Johnny to the orphanage, straight from the ship.

Between their games of bingo etc, many older couples on board just loved playing with J.J. and were in tears at the thought that this gorgeous child, now an orphan, (which he virtually was), would be met by the grandparents, who they thought knew all about him, but were also mourning the loss of his parents.

The nearer our approach to Australia the more agitated Kathleen naturally became....She told me that her parents and all her brothers would be meeting her on the quayside, but I made it quite clear to her that Johnny and I would be nowhere to be seen at that moment.

We would actually be berthed for two days, and I hoped eventually to be able to tour the Royal Melbourne Childrens Hospital, with a Dr Anderson, who was a lady I knew from the days at St Thomas'.

I planned then to embark for one last time, to Sydney on my own....

I joined the choir for the final church service on board, and the Captain thanked us all.

Off then to my cabin, for the horrible task of packing Johnny's clothes, watched a film of the Melbourne Olympiad, and another of Diana Dors, in the evening. I slept fitfully.

Next day was all go of course. There is so much for everyone to check, whether they be members of the crew or the passengers.

Customs men come aboard, baggage is everywhere, the journey has been enjoyed by most, but now everyone has had enough of the frivolity and drink, and looking forward to dry land once again.

The last day! Johnny had been awake part of the night, (perhaps he sensed something), so we both enjoyed an afternoon siesta.

We actually docked nearer 11p.m.

Father Perkins found my cabin, and dear little J.J. was sound asleep, thank goodness, as just to see a strange man in my cabin, dressed in that way, might have been very disturbing for him.

We were able to have a long pleasant chat, making arrangements for his early return the following morning, to drive us many many miles to the Orphanage.

The day dawned bright and sunny, I dressed John Joseph in his very best clothes, occupying my mind fully, in order to blot out the ghastly moments which I knew were ahead.

Certainly the majority of the passengers had left the ship, even if they were going on to Sydney the next day.

I caught a glimpse of Kathleen the previous evening, being met by her unsuspecting family. (the porthole in my cabin happened to overlook the berth in which we were tied). She looked her usual nervous timid self, with no sign of any elation at her homecoming. How very sad!

At this point, I now realised, to my great relief, that the two couples who were so keen to adopt Johnny, had actually disembarked, so that was the end of that problem, thank goodness.

I wondered how long it would be before Kathleen broached the subject to her parents?

My parents would have been absolutely horrified in the same situation, to discover that their daughter had placed a grandchild of theirs in an orphanage, but then it just would NOT have happened....

How long would it be before she even visited the child herself?

Now the 5th March 1957. Father Perkins arrived in his somewhat dilapidated banger. It was comfortable however, and we travelled over one hundred miles, through the bush, until we reached what looked more like a banana plantation!

It was, in fact, St Joseph's Foundling Hospital, at Broadmeadows, Victoria.

Bells were ringing, nuns were chanting. It was otherwise very peaceful, but incredibly hot!

THERE WERE ONE HUNDRED AND THREE BABIES THERE!!!!!

Father Perkins introduced me to Sister Gennaro.

John Joseph looked at me, but not with his usual smile. He seemed to sense that something was not quite right. He murmured Mama to me.....

A second Sister brought in tea on a tray for us, and I believe I endeavoured to make polite conversation.

Perhaps five or ten minutes later a third Sister appeared, slightly curtsied to me, gently took Johnny from my arms, and swept out of the room, as ghostlike as she had come.

I was choking. The whole thing was unreal. Like something out of a horrific nightmare, which hopefully I could shake myself out of very soon. (I find myself crying while I am writing this bit!!)

John was one year old the very next day! It was the 6thMarch.

The journey back to the ship I hardly remember, even though the Priest tried to point out the sights en route. How could I ever forget that beautiful child.

That afternoon I spent alone on the sundeck. No one interrupted my thoughts. My job was done... but my memories would go on forever....

Church Point, Sydney

View from Church Point

CHAPTER 10

The short last lap of the journey to Sydney seemed so very quiet.

All the younger crowd appeared to have left the ship at Melbourne. Stewards had received their well earned tips, and an early night was had by all, in order to rise at 6a.m. to see ourselves going through 'the heads', and so into the spectacular harbour. Of course in those days there was no Sydney Opera House to see, but the yachts were everywhere, and the larger ships were dressed overall for our arrival.

Even Macquarie Street, the equivalent of our Harley Street, looked magnificent, with its very many high-rise flats, and the Presbyterian Church of Scotland nearby.

Little did I imagine that I would be nursing a very wealthy business woman there, in the Astor Flats, in the not too distant future!

We docked an hour earlier than expected, so I was able to enjoy a last leisurely breakfast on board. Several passengers ventured to ask me how I was feeling now, but I mostly replied with a sickly grin, or found myself saying,'no comment'. In actual fact I could not bear to think about it all!

My cousin Tony, (a ship's Captain), his wife Betty, and her Father Bruce, arrived on board. Also friends of my parents, who were working temporarily in Sydney, for the General Electric Company, so we all had a celebratory drink together.

Would you believe they were arguing over whose house I should go to! Apparently Hettie and Don were planning to take me on holiday with them to Port Macquarie, at Easter, so the decision was made for me to go first to Church Point with my cousin. As we drove over the magnificent North Shore bridge, I had yet another fine view of the harbour, and the tugs busily at work.

If you remember I had given no previous thought to the looks of the baby, before I met him, and exactly the same thing happened on my arrival at the house at Church Point. The view was out of this world. The house was glass walled completely on the two front sides, situated up on a hill, and overlooking a large shimmering lake, with only three other houses some distance away in the bush. The sun was shining, and it was very hot, considering that it was now nearly Autumn. We sat drinking cold beer, talking ten to the dozen, but avoiding, for now, my experience with J.J.

The silence in the bush was remarkable, broken only by the sound of the Cicardas, Kookaburras, and Woodpeckers, and at night we fairly regularly came across the odd small black snake.

The cat brought a more colourful snake into the kitchen one evening. Tony's wife, who is truly Australian, immediately jumped on to a table, so I quickly followed , feeling sure that she must know that it was poisonous. Luckily it was a false alarm!

Everyone enjoyed telling us 'Pommies' that there were tarantulas down the loos, but luckily I never experienced that!

We fished with Bruce from a small rowing boat on the lake. Good fun, but essential to wear an old sun hat like him, as it was absolutely baking out there.

Bruce in rowing boat

I had applied for a nursing post at the Royal North Shore Hospital, so Tony drove me to see the place from the outside. I refrained, however, from telling them that I had arrived in the country, as rather fancied the idea of the holiday at Easter! They apparently liked to employ English nurses, especially those who were operating theatre trained!

Doctor Doug Tracy was arriving back from England soon, to perform Arterial Surgery at the 'North Shore', which he had learnt at St Thomas' and I was in line to be his theatre sister! On the way home we drove round a place called Denstone, and one called Eastwood, which was my surname at the time.

The 10th March was my birthday. Colin arrived in a cab at 8p.m. It was a lovely surprise, and he mixed well with everyone thank goodness. He slept the night on the couch, driving into Sydney at 6a.m. with Bruce, who was a reporter on the Sydney Morning Herald.

I am now the proud possessor of a Koala bear, a marquisite Kangaroo brooch, and a beautiful compact with the harbour bridge on it!

Surfing at Palm Beach was my next treat. At the best of times I am not a strong swimmer, but it was terrific fun. One very useful thing to remember is to NEVER EVER, under any circumstances, wear a bikini in the surf! Yes, I lost the top of mine!!!

Very exciting to collect the developed photographs from the local chemist. Some lovely ones of J.J. with all his admirers on board, and even one or two of Kathleen and I. (I prayed that one day I would be able to show all these to John.) Colin was now on 'our' ship heading for Honolulu!

By now, my cousin Tony had gone back to sea again, this time on the 'Wonganoola' to New Zealand.

A neighbour invited me on to his 'starters' motor launch for the local yacht race. Great, as there was a good wind, and even some rain.

Very soon I had a letter from Colin in Auckland. He was now assisting in the Purser's office on the ship, as someone off sick.

There was another letter from the North Shore Hospital. My interview was on Tuesday next!

Sydney is a very smart shopping centre, so Maisie, Bruce's wife, and I, spent the day there, choosing something suitable for me to wear the following week.

The day out to Katoomba I shall never forget. The famous Blue Mountains are a glorious sight, consisting of the Three Sisters, The Bride's Veil, and Leure Cascades. We rode on the scenic railway, and had lunch by a swimming pool, in a park called Blackheath.

At last a letter from Kathleen. She had obviously been to see J.J. but he is not well, and has a high temperature. (I am not surprised!) She doesn't mention whether she has told her parents yet or not, but I suspect that she hasn't.

On 24thMarch I moved from Church Point to Hettie and Don's house at Newport. They collected me in his day old Holden Special....a terrific car!

We then drove off to a Koala Reserve at Bobbin Head. These places are very superior to our English zoos, as more open plan, and spacious.

The S.S.Iberia was now in Sydney, and one of my St. Thomas' friends was ship's sister, so she invited me to a cocktail party on board the following week.

I was beginning to feel guilty with all this hospitality. It was high time that I found myself a temporary job to help pay my way. There was an Old Peoples nursing home near Het's, so I did some useful night work for a few weeks, before our holiday. It was not unusual to have tea with the undertakers!!

During May we drove 300miles to the beach at Flynn's Surf Club. We drove another 50miles to the Yarrowitch Falls. What views!

Now the playing has got to stop. Tomorrow I report for duty at The Royal North Shore Hospital!!

Brandy, Theatre Sister at The Royal North Shore Hospital

CHAPTER 11

Working with Doug Tracy again was very enjoyable. So much had happened to me, and to him, in the interim period, since we first met in Elizabeth Ward at St Thomas' in London. He was dying to hear whether Kathleen had yet taken the baby home to her parents, as you may remember, he was one of the few people who knew the correct story, in the first place.

Sadly, I told him, that I doubted if she ever would. Working in operating theatres is never easy, but somehow I had always enjoyed the surgical side of things. Stitching patients up eventually, in the knowledge that most of them would make a full recovery, and soon be home with their loved ones again.

Especially rewarding of course, were the occasional Caesarian Sections. Within minutes the baby was delivered, and to hear that faint cry was just marvellous. Behind that mask we were able to smile for a few moments!

There were quite a few English nurses working at the 'North Shore, so sometimes on night duty, whilst sterilizing and autoclaving, we were able to have a good natter about home! We were not exactly homesick, but as we all know, there is no place like home!

Actually my greatest friend turned out to be an Australian nurse called Leone. She had the most beautiful bright auburn hair I have ever seen, and she washed it at least three times a week! (It was even more red than our Sarah Ferguson's!)

Her hobby was drawing babies. Not any old babies, but round, cuddly cartoon type, pink ones, with dimples on the back of their hands. They were fantastic!

We spent our off duty hours together whenever possible, taking a taxi to the beach, to enable us to have as much time of sea air and sunshine as possible.

We both preferred shopping for clothes on our own though, so this was done when our off duty hours differed from each other.

On the 16thJune I started two months night duty. Without wishing to frighten anyone, I shall list here a few of the happenings during those hair raising times!

The very first night there were two cases right away....A young boy with a piece of metal through his hand, and the other person with a Pott's fracture of his ankle.

The second night we had a burst abdomen, and an acute obstruction....and so it goes on....

Leone, my Australian friend

The third night there was a nasty cut tendon, followed by an acute appendicectomy, and about 4a.m. an emergency Caesarian. This time, I'm afraid, the baby died, but fortunately the mother survived.

One evening, very late on, we had a dear old lady of 87yrs, who had fallen downstairs, and broken her jaw. I recall her name was Mrs Penfold, and of course she had to be 'wired up'.

This was speedily followed by a craniotomy, (lifting the skull), and later by a perforated ulcer...and so we went on...

During the day Leone was attending art classes to improve her baby cartoons, if that was possible, and I enjoyed some French language tuition in the afternoons, just for a change.

Now August, and back working in the operating theatre by day, assisting Doug again. He was now expert at repairing those burst femoral arteries!

So strange to think that he was the very one who sent me to his Father-in Law in the first place, 12,000 miles away in England!

Six months had now passed, and Betty's Mum and Dad were patiently waiting to take me on holiday with them to the outback. I certainly didn't need much persuading for this one!

Bruce's brother owned a sheep station at a place called Ryleston, and at that time there was a very serious drought. Even the swimming pool water had to be used for the animals.

Patsy and Harry were a delightful couple. The property was known as 'GRAVEE'.

As we arrived, the surrounding countryside had rather a sad appearance, purely because of the drought, but there was sure plenty of life inside that homestead!

There was an absolute mountain of empty beer bottles at the side of the house outside, which gave the game away somewhat!!

The annual sheep shearers were 'in town'. Patsy cooked enormous meals, which they devoured, and due to the incredible heat, they naturally also consumed a great deal of liquor!

My day was fantastic! I drove tractors, rode horses, fed the cows, rounded up the poor sheep who were desperately short of food and water, and sadly also helped to collect in the dead ones.

We ate fabulous food ourselves, which was all delivered by aeroplane, would you believe.

Harry had his own private pilot's licence, flew his own plane, so did the shopping!

Brandy and dog on horseback

He also flew the tourists to and from Ayers Rock,.a very strange red rock which everyone wanted to see.

Ayers Rock

You may remember the baby/dingo case there? Luckily, I believe now, that the poor Mother has been cleared of the murder of her child, as they have found fresh evidence to prove that the baby WAS killed by a wild dog!

*Brandy
and pet lamb*

Patsy and pet lamb

Patsy had a pet lamb which we all enjoyed feeding with a baby's bottle! He was not going to suffer from the drought, even though his poor mother had.

Although there was acres of dead grass, the Eucalyptus trees, and the hills surrounding the property gave plenty of colour, and in the late evening, the sunsets had to be seen to be believed!

I was therefore keen to take as many photographs as possible, and have them developed back in Sydney.

Horrors! While awaiting their development, I received an envelope from Patsy, containing the actual lens from the camera!! She had found it gleaming in the sun by the swimming pool! I have exactly ONE photograph only of Patsy and the lamb during that holiday!!

The heat was intense, but in the afternoon we fed the poor motherless lambs, and someone persuaded me to take a shot at a rabbit, but luckily I missed! I hate that sort of thing!

Even the poor kangaroos were coming out of the bush to try and find some food and water, but there was no way that I would be tempted to try and shoot one of those, especially as some had babies in their pouches.

3rd November was a beautiful day, about 100'F, but everyone praying for rain.

I drove out in the landrover with the manager Gordon, mainly spreading feed for the cattle, but still sadly also collecting in the dead sheep. We visited Old Kate's Hut, and found a creek full of red flowers called Bottle Brush.

In the evening the rain fell, breaking the drought record, so it was another excuse to celebrate. Tomorrow we were leaving Ryleston for the three hundred and fifty mile journey to Albany. We left at 5a.m. to avoid the heat, but did not reach our destination until 3.30p.m.

Bob Chalker's dairy farm was a welcome sight. The Gelahs and Cockies spoke and sang songs to us!

We had a good look round the town, taking Bob's little son in his 'bed wagon'. He had poliomyelitis five years ago.

In the evening we all went to the 'pictures' to see Harry Belafonte, and James Mason in 'Island in the Sun'.

Next morning we were off again, this time heading for 'The Little Hut' on the Murray River, where we planned to catch lobster.

Only two miles away was the famous 'Dora Dora' pub, with all its fascinating collection of weird Australian guns, extinct animals, etc etc. Alf Wright was IT! We spent some hilarious   evenings in there, meeting drovers who were moving their cattle hundreds of miles across country, but who 'parked' them between grids, from sunset to sunrise!!

We camped in the 'Hut' which was right beside the bank of the river, surrounded by Willow trees, but it was incredibly cold at night!

I can still remember wearing all the day clothes we had with us, plus any blankets we could borrow from Alf!

Instead of fishing, we landed up playing tennis at Talmalmo The funniest thing was to see Clem Jones, the drover, leaving his sixty one cattle, six dogs, two horses and a sulky, to make up the team! Later he took me for a ride in his sulky, and, as you probably know, there is only one seat!!

I think we must have caught some lobster. I can remember cooking them alive, (Ugh!) in the boiling water, on the camp fire! I couldn't do that now either!

Sheepshearing appealed to me, but I was not strong enough, and decided to watch.

We said goodbye to Alf, and left Talmalmo for Yass, staying one night at 'The Australian Hotel'. A bath at last!

On to Canberra for a few hours, before heading for home. Certainly no other capital compares with this one.   It is smart, but exceptionally small.

Many years ago, I was reading a book about Jean Batten, the famous New Zealand pilot, who flew from England to Sydney, Australia. The author of the book was Ian Mackersey, and it was called 'Garbo of the Skies'.

In it he mentions an Air Pageant, at Newcastle, North of Sydney, where some of the male pilots were, to say the least, a bit sick of Jean, and her 'high falootin' ways, so they decided to bring her down a peg or two!

In a rather dangerous fashion, two of the pilots flew low enough to keep her up in the air, while she was taking visitors up for a half hour spin in her plane. The two names mentioned were Jack Chapman, who became deputy general manager of Trans Australian Airlines, and Harry Purvis, who was one and the same Harry I stayed with on his property at 'Gravee' in Ryleston! He who flew the tourists to Ayers Rock and back, and did our food shopping for the sheep station!

He had obviously not changed one iota! Still the mad, game for anything type of bloke, but dearly loved by his wife Patsy.(with the pet lamb).and by all of us (except perhaps Jean Batten!).

Our little "wicker" house
at St. Leonards, North Shore

CHAPTER 12

My six months at the Royal North Shore Hospital had been the most valuable experience. Whatever I did in the future, this would always come in useful.

The lists had varied from assisting with the:- E.N.T.surgery, Urology, Empyemas, Craniotomies, Laminectomies, Sequestromes, Smith Petersons, Cystostomies, Thorectomies, Anterio Lobectomies, and one day I even witnessed the first attempt by a surgeon to replace a cancerous trachea, with a plastic one.

Just previous to that he had performed a Patent Ductus operation on a child. Leone phoned to say that she had found us a small artist's studio at the bottom of someone's back garden. It was in St Leonards, still on the North Shore. We could move in on the 25thNovember. Great! Temperature is now 103'F.

My next decision was to enrol with a Nursing Agency, called 'The Gordon Club'. The Matron is called Miss Collier. She trained at Aberdeen Royal, in Scotland, but is actually English she says.

Now 22nd November, - my first private patient. A Mrs Najar, in her own home in Kingsford. Has Cardiac Arrest and Diabetes. A very sick soul, and very difficult, but luckily I have the patience of JOB! Old 'pop' cooked the lunch for the housekeeper, himself and me....Lebanese cabbage rolls!

I am relieving other nurses for their day off, so the following day I found myself nursing Mrs Mark Foy's Mother, at Elizabeth Bay. She has Diverticulitis,and I worked the full twelve hours......8a.m. - 8p.m.

Quite a day, but I enjoyed every minute of it. Less hot, and a wonderful view of the harbour.

Now a more permanent job, nursing Dr Traill's wife, at the Astor Flats, in Macquarie Street, which I mentioned admiring from the ship, as we arrived through 'The Heads' in Sydney.

Little did I imagine that I would be working there! Mrs Traill has Cancer of the Oesophagus, and in fact has Carcinomatosis, which bluntly means that she is riddled with it poor soul. Beyond the stage

Leone

of treatment in hospital in fact. However her mind is still very alert, and she enjoys hiding things from the nurses on top of her wardrobe!!

The flat is magnificent, the view out of this world, and Dr Traill, being retired, likes to prepare superb meals for us all, especially fish dishes. He purchases king sized prawns, and lobsters, and delights in showing us all how to tackle them, even to using the special silver pick, to dig out the juicy bits!

Poor Mrs Traill tries to eat, but invariably chokes on the slightest morsel.

Sydney is a wonderful exciting place and so much to do there. I actually attended the Church of Scotland service at St Stephen's Presbyterian Church, down the road, in Macquarie Street, where ear pieces are provided for the hard of hearing.

Drive in cinemas are twice nightly with one interval, and milk bars are at every few yards it seems.

Brandy

Pedestrians walk on the left hand side of the pavement in the direction in which they are heading.

29th November Leone and I moved house into our cute little studio. It had been built especially for her artist son. He had made good use of it, but had now moved on to bigger and grander places.

All the furniture was wicker, with a huge wicker blind separating the lounge from the bedroom. Colourful chintz curtains. Hot and cold running water, absolutely essential for Leone's constant hair washing!!

We adored it, and our landlady was actually called...Mrs Shore!!

She too loved having us there, now that her son had flown the nest, and her husband had passed away.

My patient Mrs Traill requiring oxygen now, and her husband is very nervous and upset, but Mrs T. refuses to go to hospital. I asked permission to work right through the seven days, to give him support, but of course other nurses take over from me at night.

7th December I was invited to an Hawaiian barbecue at Mosman, another very pleasant area, so I made myself a superb sarong in

Hawaiian material. I met a salesman from Scotland, and a great evening was had by all.

Another seven days with Mrs Traill, and then I really did think I needed a break, so Leone and I decided to go to a drive-in. The film was 'The Robe' with Jean Simmons,and Victor Mature. Excellent!

S.S.Strathmore was in port, so I invited Liz Rogers for dinner. She was ship's sister, and had been with me at 'Tommy's'.

On the 20th December she invited me to a dance on the ship, but the temperature was now 107', the hottest day since 1939 apparently, so it was cancelled.

Mrs Traill now very serene and comfortable at the moment, which is rather rewarding for all that her nurses have gone through during the last few months.

The following day I was invited on board with Liz and her fellow officers for lunch. Temperature now a little more reasonable.

Christmas day was 100ºF and I offered to prepare dinner for the Traills, and a friend of theirs. We had several cocktails and champagne, so it became easier as I progressed, and a good time was had by all!!

Late that afternoon, I set out for Church Point, which is quite a long way, and very little public transport, but I had insisted that Tony and Betty didn't come to collect me, not knowing exactly what time I would manage to leave the Traills. This would also mean breaking into their own Christmas festivities. Having only managed a bus to Mona Vale, I set off on a very hot trek!!

The last thing I had thought to bring was a hat, but I very nearly collapsed with the heat, especially in the dips of the road, which of course were deserted. I even saw a snake!

After all that champagne earlier in the day, I was absolutely parched, but no water in sight, except for the mirage covering the stinking hot road in front of me, which gave the impression of water.

My luck was in, as they say, as just when I was about to sink to my knees, and to certainly drop everybody's presents, a car approached, and the driver, being a friend of Tony's, recognised me. Without hesitation he turned the car round, and whizzed me off to Church Point. The entire evening was hilarious, and my favourite present was a pair of black baby doll pyjamas, in which I pranced around to the amusement of all!

I decided to have some tennis coaching in the new year, as that had always been my favourite sport, and my best, so on the 6th January I found myself at Chatswood, with six others, using the 'ball' machine. It was 10/- a night, and worth every penny.

That evening I received a lovely letter from my friend, Pat Murray who was now a House Doctor. He had been accepted for the Midwifery post at St Thomas' and of course was delighted.

The New Year now, and I am still nursing Mrs Traill. Every morning I pick up dozens of dividend slips, which land on the front doormat from the postman. Sugar shares, oil shares, you name it, she owned it!

She asked me to buy her a new dressing gown in David Jones, which is a marvellous store, so I took the opportunity to have a good look round while I was there.

Sydney generally is an excellent shopping centre, and the women shoppers come from miles around. They all look and dress fantastic too, just like Patsy, when she comes to town for a few days from the outback.

I receive an amazing number of letters each week, mainly from the U.K. but this time it was from Clem Jones, the drover, at Hilston, and he was almost illiterate!

Leone's romance with Henry, (Henrikkson), was not going too well, but he, and another Icelandic friend called Olaf, gave us a great evening out at 'Chequers', a Sydney night club. The floorshow was excellent, but I, unfortunately, and stupidly, ate too much, and was violently sick in the ladies loo! Most unlike me!

Erskine Church

We liked the idea of attending the Presbyterian Church, at Crow's nest, near where we were living. I had been a member of the Church of Scotland since my teenage years back in a small place called Erskine, in Renfrewshire, Scotland.

The Queen Mother was now in New Zealand, and Harold McMillan and his wife were here in Sydney for a few days.

CHAPTER 13

Very rarely am I ill, but I developed raging toothache, so off to the dentist at Crow's Nest. The Xray showed my usual huge teeth with hooked roots, not easily extracted, so he suggested a Macquarie Street specialist, as soon as it could be arranged. (These days they cut the top off the tooth, prise the gum, and remove each root separately, finally stitching the gap.) Painless under local anaesthetic!

On February 3rd I had the tooth extracted, but all in one yank, and then the gum stitched! It was well done, but I had a pretty rough week afterwards.

Meantime poor Mrs Traill was becoming steadily worse, and more bad tempered with her nurses, purely due to her condition, even arguing over the time of her injections etc.

In fact, driving us all quite mad over the most trivial of things, and still hiding allsorts ,on top of her wardrobe!

I decided it was time I moved on, and the Nursing Agency agreed with me.

On the 19thFebruary, Ash Wednesday, I arrived at St Luke's private hospital, at 8.a.m. I was asked to look after a Mrs Beattie with a Cataract. She was a Doctor's wife, and off to the operating theatre at 9a.m. I was introduced to the specialist, Mr Gregory Roberts, who knew our Mr Penman, in London.

Mr Roberts was obviously impressed by the work done at St.Thomas', and spoke very highly of Mr Penman, who was one of the world's leading eye specialists.

He pointed and joked about my Nightingale badge, which of course I always wore on my uniform, with great pride!

The Nightingale Badge,
St Thomas's Hospital,
London SE1

51

This private hospital was at Palm Beach, and the rooms were very grand. Our salaries were good too, so I should imagine that the patient's pay a bomb to have treatment there.

The following day my patient had to be kept very quiet and still, but I enjoyed meeting her daughters outside in the garden in the afternoon. One was a Doctor/Journalist, and the other an artist/housewife. I finished work at 6p.m.

Next day the Queen Mother was in Sydney, the weather sunny but windy.

Mrs Beattie's daughter asked me to stay on with her Mother for another two days, which was quite a compliment, as her Mother was up and about all ready, and reading so soon.

I enjoyed a lovely shopping spree on the following Monday, and actually saw the Queen Mother twice!

In the evening I played tennis.

Matron rang to say that there was another 'Cataract', this time a Mr Wilson at Winston Private Hospital, at Darling Point. 8 a.m.- 8 p.m.

This dear man was ninety-one, a property owner from the outback. He also had his operation at 9 a.m. but afterwards his temperature soared to 103°F and he was extremely poorly for the rest of the day. We nurses were exceptionally tired too, due to the extreme humidity.

On the fifth day after his operation, Mr Wilson accidentally hit his eye, and Dr Pittar found it necessary to redress his eye in the theatre. We were all very upset, but from then on improvement continued, thank goodness.

10th March, my birthday again, so Leone and I went to see 'The Bridge Over The River Kwai'.

Not another word from Kathleen, although I had written to her many times.

It is beginning to sound monotonous, but my third case was also a 'Cataract'. That is the joy of nursing however, as every case, and patient, are different of course. This time it was a Mr Maurice Zucherman, an Insurance Broker. He was younger, the operation a success, and my work was done.

Matron now rang to say that there were three sisters off sick, at St Luke's, on the second floor, and would I take over at midday until 10p.m! Luckily I seemed to manage quite well, with the assistance of the Deputy Matron!

Matron thanked me personally, I met no end of specialists, and poor Mrs Beattie was readmitted with a stitch left in, over her left eye!

Over the next few weeks I nursed several other ladies, including a Miss Chapman at St Luke's, a Mrs Playfairs at the Scottish Hospital, and Mrs Beattie, yet again, this time with a secondary glaucoma!

Tremendous excitement....I have booked my passage home! This time on an Italian ship called T.V.Sydney.

Mrs B says she knows the Captain....Leopaldi, nicknamed 'Poldi'!

Matron called yet again, asking me to stay, in order to nurse the Archbishop of Sydney, (no less), but unfortunately I shall be sailing on the 7thApril. Quite an honour though eh!

Absolutely no word from Kathleen to take home with me. I am desperately disappointed about that, but nothing I can do about it, as not allowed to personally contact the Orphanage.

We shall not even sail via Melbourne, on the way home, as heading up to the Barrier Reef, and Queensland, and then on to Djakarta, to pick up Dutch Indonesians!

My memories of Australia will be many and varied, but each will hold a very sacred place in my heart. I am sure the 'Aussies' really do like the 'pommies', but love 'taking the mickey' out of them, and their accent!

The 'Orcades' arrived from England with Alan Porter from 'Tommies' on board. He was ship's surgeon, so more drinks on the house, and I was able to obtain a great deal of news of all the folks back home. I didn't feel 12,000 miles away I must say!

Even when I assisted a Mr Lawes with his list of varicose veins, in the operating theatre, I found he was full of praise for a surgeon called Mr Cockett, back at St Thomas'...... I knew him well.

One of the loveliest memories I have, are the magnificent views from each, and every one, of the private nursing homes I worked in. Rose Bay, Bondi Beach, Double Bay, Bay View, and Vaucluse, to name but a few. What marvellous scenery!

Other places spring to mind like the Koala Reserve at Bobbin Head, and the Easter Show with its buck and steer riding....I could go on and on, and the weather is just the icing on the cake, in the Spring and the Summer. Winter isn't too bad either!

One devastating problem in the heat, is the bush fires, which sweep uncontrollably through the trees and dry shrub land. The wild animals and birds, and even the kangaroos, are unable to escape fast enough with their young, and the koalas suffer from terrible burns in the Eucalyptus trees.

CHAPTER 14

Quay No1.10p.m. Accompanied by several nurses, Mrs Shore, and her son Don, but not Leone, as she had flown off to Iceland with her fiancé Henry.(at last!)

We persuaded Betty and Tony not to come all the way from Church Point, just to say goodbye, but we spoke on the phone. The whole area was seething with Italians, not unnaturally, I suppose, being an Italian ship.

The ship was decorated overall again, with the usual streamers from ship to shore and back again. A brass band was in full swing, and a lone pipe major was endeavouring to serenade any odd Scotsman,(or woman!), on board!

We sailed at 10.30p.m.

Mentally I was trying to remind myself that this was a ONE class ship, and NOT to be compared with our lovely outward bound 1st class S.S.Orion, with all its trimmings!

I had accepted a single booking in a cabin for EIGHT, so you can imagine that the first thing I wanted to do was to check out my fellow travellers!!

Four adult Italians, two Maltese, myself, and two children!!! All were sick in the first two days, but everyone preferred to be on deck rather than the confines of that cabin!!

No one was using the dining room at this stage, which must be a problem for the chefs and the stewards, but as it is probably the norm at the beginning of each cruise, they no doubt have a contingency plan. I doubt if the crew are sick too, as so used to the sea, so I expect they enjoy double helpings of everything!

Thank goodness I was not accompanying a patient of any kind on this ship! It would take me all my time to look after myself, I should imagine, especially with all these Italians on board!!!

Crossing the Line ceremony

We spent one day at Brisbane, and then on via the Great Barrier Reef, which was magnificent, but no one told us that it sometimes also rains even in Queensland! It was bucketing down!

Now nine days to Djakarta, where five hundred Dutch Indonesians were embarking! I guess we had better make the most of the next eight days! I am sharing a table with a Physiotherapist and his wife.

We all wrote letters to post from Thursday Island.

Someone selected me for the Sports Committee, which included making arrangements for the Crossing the Line Ceremony!!

... more of Crossing the Line

The M.C. was endeavouring to persuade people to dance in the evening, and, as the band played the Charleston, I was swept off my feet by an enthusiastic passenger. We were so successful at it together, that we landed up giving a demonstration!

My partner was called Graham... one day to become my husband!!

Graham was the 'Judge' at the crossing the line ceremony. Six of us, three men and three women, dressed in home made grass skirts, did 'The Can Can'!

We were all then tossed into the pool, after the initiation ceremony, consisting of a bucket full of whitewash, eggs and tomatoes!

... and more!!

Finally we were presented with our 'certificates', and a very good time was had by all (especially the onlookers!).

The view from the Islands from the upper decks was fantastic, and the gale had subsided.

Friday the 18thApril we arrived at Djakarta, but no one was allowed off the ship. We were not immunised against certain diseases, but the five hundred coming aboard had been, and were apparently no threat to us thank goodness.

I couldn't admit that I liked the idea of having all these extra people on board, and jumped at the chance when the ship's Doctor invited me to his air conditioned cabin for afternoon tea on 'A' deck. There was only one snag.....we had to speak in either French or Italian!

Next day we arrived at Singapore at 7.30a.m. but were not allowed to disembark until the following morning for some unknown reason. Lucky for me, as I had developed a stinking cold, probably due to being flung in the water in a gale! I was not feeling at all sociable!

However the next afternoon I had a really hot curry in a Singapore restaurant with Graham and a guy called Peter, and somehow it seemed to be the cure! The curry was so hot that the waiter gave us all ice cold flannels with which to sponge our faces!

Me in Singapore

Graham was now leaving the ship to travel through India. He had asked me to look after some suits and some English money for him, so quite a crafty move for us to meet up again one day I thought! It would have been fun to have visited Raffles Hotel, but beyond our means I'm afraid.

We all had strict instructions to be back on board by 4p.m. which was far too early really. The ship sailed at 9.30p.m.

The ship's Doctor appeared to be even more interested in me once he realised Graham had left the ship!!

His name was Guisseppi Macaldi, first cousin of Rossano Brazzi, the film star, or so he said!

One small thing that gave him great delight was checking that my smallpox vaccine had taken! I had insisted on having it done in my thigh, because, as you probably know, it leaves an unsightly scar on one's arm!

I missed Graham terribly in the evenings, especially as he was such a good dancer. He was also a great joker, and generally very sociable.

The weather was incredibly hot at this stage, so I decided to accept the Doctor's offer, and use his cabin in the afternoons. My cabin was so crowded and unhealthy as you can imagine.

He was seldom there, but left instructions for me to have ice cold lemon juice laid on. Eventually I spent the least possible time down on the lower decks.

We reached Colombo on the 24thApril at 4p.m. A very attractive harbour with the 'Arcadia' in port.

A group of us decided to hire a car, and have a three-hour tour, visiting the Buddha's Temple, the Cinnamon Garden, and Mount Lavinia, where all the gorgeous homes are situated. The climate was perfect, and so also was the meal at the Fountain Café.

One day later we stopped at Cochin, but only for a few hours, which was more than enough, as a much poorer place, and not much to see. Having watched the primitive fishing nets, and the primitive boys diving deep for our coins, we were glad to leave.

There is never a dull moment on board ship, and this time it was the death of a Bishop who had embarked at Djakarta. This necessitated a burial at sea which we all watched!

We formed a 'Lyon's Club' to make money for charity.

We started a keep fit class on the 'forward' deck, much to the amusement of the Captain, and his fellow officers, on the bridge!

We swam, played deck quoits, and of course tried to learn Italian. Luigi, the liason officer, spoke five languages fluently, AND read Greek!!

Having now arrived in the Gulf of Aden, it is extremely hot, but as the fancy dress ball is on Friday next, several of us pressed on making the kilts with crepe paper.

In between times I did some geometry problems with a fellow passenger, and listened to another playing Strauss rather beautifully.

The "Congo"

Mario, from the Purser's office, tells me that his Grandfather was conductor of an orchestra in Italy.

Well we won first prize in our kilts, and a great night was had by all. We were presented with a bottle of Cora, which is Italian champagne. Some friends won second prize as a prehistoric monster! Imagination on board has to be seen to be believed!

The childrens' fancy dress was just as exciting.

Fancy Dress
in paper kilts

CHAPTER 15

We arrived in the Suez Canal today. It was all very exciting! From the general atmosphere, to the camels, veiled women, a Sphinx, and oxen ploughing the fields.

Egyptians moving sand by hand, and even squatting, in full view of the ship and passengers, to perform their ablutions!

Looking after children and a dog in the Suez Canal

By this time I was very short of money, so sadly I offered to babysit for a young couple, while they toured the Pyramids.

Between you and me, I regret that to this day, as still have been unable to see them. How I should love to have seen Cairo. The weather was cool and very pleasant.

Leaving Port Said at 2a.m. we were now heading for Malta. It was now cold, and due to some anti- British campaign there at that time, only the few Maltese passengers who were disembarking, were allowed to leave in a small motor launch.

As with Cairo, I was bitterly disappointed, as might never come this way again.

7th May, we arrived in Messina, in Sicily. A delightful city, clean, and bright like the weather.

The famous gold clock tower was well worth seeing, with its figuerines weaving in and out.

Then on to Taormina, to see the amazing open air Greek theatre, with Mount Etna in the background. Incidentally, the cassata ice cream was scrumptious!

Now 7a.m.on the 8thMay. We find ourselves in Napoli, able to join the excursion to Pompeii, and to see Mount Vesuvius. We visited the home of the Cameo, and of course I couldn't resist purchasing the ear rings! I couldn't afford the brooch to match!

Some of my friends left for Capri at this point, but most of us are heading for Genoa.

This brought back fond memories to me, of the trip Tish and I made to Venice on a Vespa for a bet while we were at St Thomas'. As we had left the town of Genoa, heading for Mantua and Padua, the local lads were just leaving their factory jobs for home, on their scooters. They immediately recognised us as two English girls, because we rode astride the 'bike', whereas their local girls would have been sidesaddle. To our horror, they escorted us, en masse, in their hundreds, out of Genoa! Very very funny for them, but somewhat unnerving for us!

One final day in Italy. A lovely meal of prawns and pizza, a look at the gorgeous clothes in the shops, and an art gallery in the late afternoon. We then climbed aboard the train for Paris. All slept like logs!!

On to Calais, and then the ship to Dover.

Sent telegrams to warn our families of our pending arrival in London. (No mobile phones in those days!)

There was my dear old Dad, patiently waiting for me, and a taxi then took us to my parent's new home in Hampshire.

A great deal had been happening in my absence.

A letter awaiting my arrival from Graham in Thailand, but sadly still not a word from Kathleen in Australia.

Oh how I wish there was some news of dear little J.J. It was no use, I should never be able to erase the memory of that dear little chap from my mind.

I promised myself there and then, that I would spend the rest of my life trying to find out what had happened to him, and if he was safe and happy now.

Within weeks, I had written to the Orphanage, and to Kathleen's homestead, without of course mentioning the baby, but it was to no avail in both cases.

Staying at home in the country, in a bungalow with my parents, was,to me, a complete anticlimax, after the life I had been living for the past two years.

Very shortly I joined two of my old nursing friends in their flat at Victoria, London SW1.

Certainly I wanted a complete change, so for two weeks I worked in the model suit department at Selfridges!!

On the 30thJune, I commenced a part time job in the Casualty Dept. of the Westminster Childrens Hospital, (now Chelsea and Westminster), in order to allow me to attend a model course, (just for fun) at the Dubarry Academy, in Piccadilly.

St Thomas' asked me back as a night sister, but I declined the offer, as, although a great honour, I just never did like night work, even though I had done my fair share of it over the years.

In retrospect, my life was to take so many more different and interesting turns, that I am glad now that I did not do that.

Before leaving Hampshire, Pat Murray, now an Obstetrician, took me out for a Devon tea in his faithful old 'banger' called Jose.

On our return home I found another letter from Graham, informing me that he was flying home from India that day!! He had been very ill with Dysentry, so his planned trip around India was cancelled!

My trunk had also arrived at Camberley Station.

Seemed quite strange to be nursing 10a.m.-4p.m. and to be learning about grooming, makeup, exercising, hair, etc. etc. in the evenings. I was told to pluck my eyebrows in the centre!

The hairdresser was excellent. He suggested that I wear my hair longer, flat on top, but with a piece curling forward to balance my nose! (I still have to do that!)

Now the mannequin parade! Each one of us had to be shown how to walk, and it was apparently better if we wore three and a half inch heels!!!!!

One evening, I was giving my flat mates, Anita and Jackie, a demonstration of all this, when one heel broke off completely, and I fell from top to the bottom of the staircase! Anita has since reminded me that my legs were so bruised, and the finals next day, that I smothered them with foundation makeup!! The photographic session was in The Charles Adam's Studios at 83, Duke Street, where I learnt all about different lighting and cameras.

The following week, the actual photographs of us were taken!

Brandy at Model School!

CHAPTER 16

Most of us know that living and working in the big city can be marvellous fun, and even on a Sunday one can combine going to a good church service at St Martin's in the Fields, a visit to the Tate Gallery, and perhaps a walk through Belgravia to Knightsbridge, with an enjoyable coffee at somewhere like the El Cubano at the end of it.

On Monday evening we were taught how to handle an umbrella on the catwalk! Quite tricky! The Principal and Supervisor were there.

You may have noticed at this point that I am not describing my job at the Westminster Childrens Hospital. That is purely because in a Childrens Casualty Department it is mostly rather sad, and often quite 'gory', so I am sparing the reader most of the details. Even a five week old baby was brought in dead yesterday.

Thursday and Friday were dress rehearsal, and finals night at the Academy, so you can imagine the 'girlish' excitement that prevailed! I wore a glamorous ice blue long evening dress, and for the photo session, a sleeveless sweater and shorts! It was all tremendous fun, but a bit nerve racking to say the least! Joan Wells won the prize for the most promising model. (I wonder whatever happened to her over the years?)

Perhaps, after all, I should stick to nursing!!!

A Doctor called Wilfred Leach invited me to The Players Theatre, situated under Charing Cross Bridge. The Victorian atmosphere was terrific, and after the show, we were all allowed to dance on the stage until the early hours.

Another good night was had by all at the Albert Hall. It was a 'Prom' night, with Sir John Barbirolli, and the Hallé Orchestra. It was a Viennese theme with his wife playing the oboe.

All during the summer months, Graham continued to write to me from the North of England, where he was working, and occasionally he would come down to see me. The phone calls were numerous!

Tuesday 9th September was a beautiful day, so I walked through the park to the bank. On the way, I stopped to buy a Daily Telegraph, reading the block ad. job vacancies for nurses.

An Industrial Nurse was required for shift work at Mars Ltd in Slough, the makers of all sorts of sweets, and the famous Mars Bar, but somehow I was always under the impression that no one was ever lucky enough to acquire jobs from these newspaper block advertisements... I thought the block ads were fictitious, but something made me decide to apply anyway.

That afternoon Matron and I had afternoon tea with Lord Shackleton of Burwood, on the roof garden at Derry and Toms. I think he was a former patient, but I cannot quite remember the details of that.

I was tremendously excited about my forthcoming interview at Mars Ltd. Both factory and offices are very modern, and the Surgery, where I would be working, was a joy to behold.

Naturally they worked a shift system there, and my hours would be either 6a.m.-2p.m, 2p.m. -10p.m., or 10p.m.-6a.m. with three days off in between. I was told that I would take my meals with the managers.

I was given a very thorough medical examination and declared 'disgustingly healthy'!!

Monday 15th September I received the great news that I had been successful, and that the job was mine. The Personnel Officer promised to look for digs for me in the Slough area.

The 29th September was my first day, bewildering as all new jobs are, but extremely interesting, and, as I was shown each department, I spoke to literally hundreds of staff. The chaps in the factory just love a new nurse to tease, and the banter was flying!

It was a delight being so near Windsor, and I thoroughly enjoyed occasionally going to the Theatre Royal, which was situated immediately opposite the Castle on the hill.

Mars Ltd was always busy, day and night, but so well organised and safety conscious, that the treatments we gave were on the whole mainly for colds and coughs, headaches, hangovers! skin dryness causing sugar dermatitis, or even depression sometimes, for something happening at home. The main thing was to keep the workers happy and working, as some of the tasks on the machines were very repetitive.

Maintenance men were at more risk, having some heavy object or other fall on them from a great height! Dressings, or even stitches being the order of the day. We had one strange chap who used to 'talk' to the sweets in the 'Tunes' Department!

Some of the ladies had romance problems, or worries about their children at home, so we acted as councillors as well!

I had my own problems too! A Doctor, and a manager asked me out, but I discovered that both were married, so politely declined both offers. Testing me I expect!!

On one occasion I did a double shift, when a colleague's fiance died suddenly. After sixteen hours it was me who was ready to drop!!

During December, I received masses of Christmas cards, and Koala bears everywhere, but sadly STILL no word from Kathleen. I knew the orphanage was not allowed to contact me.

By April 1959,I had been introduced socially to the Managing Director of Berlei (U.K.) Ltd the 'Berlei Bra' company. Mr Keith Burley, (yes, spelt this way), was an absolutely marvellous, down to earth Australian. Full of life and vigour, and expected all his fellow workers to act likewise!

For many weeks he tried to persuade me, in pubs usually at lunchtime, to become his Personnel Manager. I explained that I was a qualified nurse, and had no Personnel qualifications.

However, he won the day eventually, by suggesting that I took the job, and then attended two years at night school to learn Personnel Management! I passed the exams!! (In this day and age this would certainly NEVER be allowed!)

It was an offer too good to refuse...

I left Mars, crossed from one side of the Slough Trading Estate to the other, and started work. No night duty, or shift work and an even greater salary, but plenty of very hard work, even to organizing the Social Club, and the Christmas parties for both children and adults!

The real reason for my being offered the job, was because a new law had been passed by the government, stating that any factory having more than a certain number of employees, must now have a qualified State Registered Nurse at the helm, to replace any first aid nurse, which had been the norm up until then.

Again, as at Mars Ltd, there were very few major accidents, even with the maintenance staff, but with sewing machines, and perhaps the odd person with Epilepsy, there was always that slight risk. Needles through fingers were more common, especially in the design department!

I must say I felt extremely honoured when I discovered that there had been thirty applicants for this position, but of course it was the nursing qualifications which sealed it!

There were nearly a thousand employees, one very large open plan office, plus several smaller ones, and five factories, although granted, some of these were situated in Wales.

There was no one senior to me in the Personnel Department, so I had complete freedom to organise as I wished, with the help of a very capable secretary called Betty Shepherd, who years earlier, had won a National newspaper competition, to become 'Secretary of the Year'!!

I had absolutely no idea how to type in those days, let alone use a word processor, or a computer, as I do now!

During my five odd years at 'Berlei', I married Graham, and within two years I had given birth to a wonderful bouncing boy called Scott.

The Personnel Department was left in the capable hands of Betty, who was there umpteen years later, and became my son's Godmother.

After four years at home, my feet began to 'itch' again. My son was very happy at his pre-prep school, but I didn't fancy returning to nursing. Somehow the same magic started to work for me... there was a small shop in our village High St, which became vacant, and eventually became mine... for sixteen successful years!!

My Boutique, for men, women and eventually children as well, grew like topsy, and was my pride and joy, second only to my husband and son of course.

I had part time help while Scott was small, but soon I managed to cope on my own, and it was called 'Brandy', which is my Christian nickname. It was not a name the public could forget!

In time, I made many, many, hundreds of friends, and never a day goes past now, without someone acknowledging me by my nickname, in the village High Street, or telling me that they still wear the evening dress or bra they bought from me all those years ago!!

CHAPTER 17

By 1966 I could wait no longer. I must find out what has happened to John Joseph, and also Kathleen for that matter.

I wrote to Father Perkins, and to the St Joseph's Foundling Hospital in East Melbourne, Australia.

The replies were as expected.....JOHN JOSEPH HAD BEEN ADOPTED.

Originally he was placed in the care of temporary foster parents, with his real Mother having access to him, during this time.

It only lasted a couple of months, and then Kathleen, who had given much thought to it, they said, and had discussed every aspect thoroughly with the Director of the Bureau, finally decided to sign a consent for his adoption. UGH!

Accordingly, on the 7th July1957, the same year that we had travelled from England, 'John was placed with a very fine Catholic couple on the land in Victoria'.

These people are apparently well known to the Reverend Father Perkins, who himself had chosen this home for him. The Father, an old public schoolboy, and grazier, 'promised to give John every educational advantage, and all that he would require from life'. (I now know from John himself, that he was treated as a labourer, working sometimes up to fifteen hours a day!) He still has back trouble!

This man had previously adopted two girls, who became 'sisters' to John, (now being called Peter), and that is why he was known to Father Perkins!

Where are you now John Joseph? I would so dearly love to hear from you? You must be thirty years old, and perhaps have children of your own?

My son is 24, an Old Etonian, and working for an Audio/Visual company near Heathrow Airport.

I have closed the Boutique now, after sixteen successful years, and teaching an Arab girl here to speak English, in her own home. There are nine children, and two wives! Sometimes we are distracted by the Koran, pop music or a baby yelling! Even a huge heated family row sometimes breaks out, but whatever, it is a fascinating part time job in my later years!

I have only one wish left..... to meet and to hold J.J. in my arms once more!

In 1987 my mind was again working overtime, and I started a private Domestic Cleaning Agency in this area. People were advertising for help in their homes, and others were looking for work, so I was able to piece the two together. Fourteen years on, it is still going strong!

CHAPTER 18

In February 1996 I asked my niece, and her husband in Melbourne, if they could possibly contact the Catholic Welfare Bureau, in East Melbourne, for me, to enquire about J.J.

Times have changed radically now, and an adopted child has the legal right to search for his or her original parents, (but not of course the nurse who may have escorted them from one country to another, when they were under a year old!)

Back came the reply, from a Ms Rosemarie Slater, in the Adoption Information Service, to my niece Joan, to say that I was NOT a blood relation of his!! However my interest would be placed on file until such times that the child wished to make an application to contact me!

TO DATE THEY HAD NO CONTACT WITH HIM!!!

In May 1996 a certain Miss Geraldine Morgan at the Catholic Welfare Bureau, apparently interviewed a 'John McGrath', and he was allowed to pass a message via them to me!

9th June 1996

I shall never forget that day! I received a long, hand written letter from John Joseph, now called Peter Kirby, telling me all about himself and his family. He has a wife called Leanne, and two children called Madeline and Aiden, some dogs, and some horses.

As you can imagine, I was over the moon, so packed up a huge parcel of the story so far, plus all the relevant photographs of us, and Kathleen, (his mum) on board ship, and sent them by registered mail to Peter in Melbourne.

I added a note saying, wait until the children are in bed, pour a neat Scotch for Leanne and yourself, and be prepared to have a good cry!!

1st July 1996   We spoke on the phone at last!!

Reading the story, he said, he finds it very hard to believe it is all about him! He had never seen a photograph of himself at that age until then, and he was not only surprised that he had travelled all that way on a ship, but that he WAS AUSTRALIAN!!

He has decided not to tell his adoptive parents, but will tell 'his two sisters', Geraldine and Adrian. His wife Leanne, who is a nurse, is planning to check the Electoral Roll for a Kathleen Mary McGrath.

Peter's air letter to me on the 2nd July says that he wishes he could give me that big hug that I yearn to have!

How like the stories told on the Cilla Black 'Surprise, Surprise' show, I thought.

After "Surprise, Surprise", April 1997

CHAPTER 19

Tuesday 29th April 1997

My son Scott and his wife Gill, had invited Graham and I to dinner, in their home in Chiswick Quay. London.W4. Nothing unusual in that I hear you say.

I am still running the cleaning business, and take calls in the evenings, so found myself saying to Scott on the phone, that I really wish he wouldn't arrange for me to go to London during the week. They had one baby Max at the time, but had a nanny, so I was more needed at weekends anyway.

Under the circumstances, unbeknown to me, I think poor Scott nearly had a heart attack, and rushed to ask Graham to be sure to get me there exactly on time.

The nanny was cooking a WOK meal for us all, and we all ate it in the lounge, in front of the T.V., which I thought rather strange, as so many of us, and the table was there in the open plan kitchen, cum dining room, cum lounge. All very pleasant, with a fantastic view of all the private yachts in the Marina.

My family had just returned from a trip to Australia, with Max, so it seemed quite natural , and a good opportunity for them to show me the video.

My plate was whisked from me by the nanny, before I had time to finish the last morsel.

The phone rang on my left, and Scott answered it. (Normally that phone was never situated just there!) He passed it to me, saying that the call was for me. I remember replying that 'no one knows I am here'!

Little did I know.....the 'world' knew that I was there!

The T.V. switched to Cilla's 'Surprise Surprise' programme at the L.W.T. studios, and Cilla herself was talking to me on the telephone!

We were situated on the 1st floor of the house, as the ground floor contains the playroom, and a very spacious garage.

Graham and Peter (J.J.)

Suddenly, several men dashed up the staircase from the garage, clutching lights, cameras, and microphones! I thought we had been raided!

Cilla was asking me all sorts of questions about 'the baby' etc, and calling me Brenda, which I absolutely hate!!

The studio audience were treated to a gorgeous shot of Max, my grandson, lying in his Mother's arms, and in unison said aaahhh!

All I could think of was that I had kicked off my shoes before the meal, and that my hair probably needed combing, and I could do with some lipstick!

Then the real shock! She told me to look to my right, where Peter, yes, J.J. was standing!! I leapt up to have that longed for hug! Absolutely unbelievable!......and a man now of course!

Many months before, unbeknown to me, a researcher had come down to one of my neighbours. Wendy was a freelance hairdresser at that time, and together they arranged for me to pop over there while 'a customer' was having her hair done, to advice her on buying a cat for her disabled mother!' I adore cats, and have four of my own, so believe it or not, I typed out a long list of do's and dont's of buying a cat for a disabled person!

In Brandy's garden after "Surprise, Surprise"
showing Peter even more photographs
of himself as a baby.

This enabled the researcher to decide whether I would, a) cope with the shock, and b) be able to tell the story clearly etc. My son insisted that no way would I go in to an ITV studio, with a live audience, so the decision was made to record it from his home. The lights failed at one point during the recording, but were restored from the Marina I think.

The next two hours or so were very exciting, as we ALL climbed into a huge limousine which held at least ten or more, and drove over to the actual LWT studio bar to meet Cilla herself. I had no idea that Peter and Leanne had been in London for a whole week before, staying in one of the best hotels, enjoying the sights of the big city, all at LWT's expense!

Peter even managed to find his birth certificate in London. Next day, my son took the day off, and drove them to my home here in Burnham, in Buckinghamshire. We then toured Windsor and the Castle, having lunch near The Long Walk.

Brandy Thomas

Leanne and Peter
November 1988

Madeline, 7yrs

Peter and Aiden, 4 years

CHAPTER 20

I think it was August that year, before the programme was eventually shown on ITV as part of the series, and I hastily asked all my friends to video it!

My son and his family were abroad again, and at that point I still didn't possess a video machine! I watched it entirely on my own, with the tears streaming down my cheeks, reliving the experience all over again. It was truly........'A Voyage of a Lifetime'.

Within days I was able to pack up and send a copy of the video to Peter and Leanne.

Apart from frequent phone calls from both ends, we now had a lull, whilst recovering from the whole drama and shock of it all.

While we were having photographs taken with Cilla that evening at LWT, Peter and Leanne were able to use Gill's mobile phone, and speak to the grandparents and their two children in Australia.

It was a very strange feeling, looking round that room by the bar, realising that all those people had seen me on T.V., but I knew nothing about any of them, until I saw the actual video!

T'Pau was on my programme, someone who I had always enjoyed, so was delighted when she came over to shake my hand, while I was speaking to Cilla.

I am 5' 71/2" tall, but much to my suprise, Cilla appeared to be even taller. Perhaps it was her high heels. She talked about my lovely grandchild, and wished her three boys would get a move on! Cilla has since lost her husband, but she is now back wowing the public all over again, mostly on 'Blind Date'

Meanwhile, Leanne had been doing her homework, and had found Kathleen, who is now 79yrs, and living in a smart private nursing home in Kew, which is in Melbourne.

It would be a long drive for them, but not impossible to visit her one day.

They were able to talk to the Matron, and later to a niece, who had had the task of clearing Kathleen's belongings from her home when she moved out.

It was she who discovered something that no one in the family had known previously (except that one brother who gave her the money to sail to England) ..... that Kathleen had had a child, and there were the photographs to prove it!

She had married eventually, but there were no children. They had separated, and her husband had since died, so virtually Peter is her next of kin! Her surname had been Johnson.

28thMay 2,000. Matron invited Peter, Leanne,and Madeline, the eldest child, to lunch with Kathleen, and it was apparently marvellous to see her coming to life, while sitting next to her newly found granddaughter! They talked about their horses, past and present, and Kathleen called Peter, J.J. and John!

Kathleen had five brothers, but only the one knew of her plight, taking money from a family trust to enable her to travel to England. Strangely, all the other brother's wives at that time had also been pregnant, so Peter has now found that he has many cousins, and is apparently the spitting image of some!!

Sharon, is the niece, who cleared Kath's house, and found to her dismay, all the details, and photographs, which had been hidden away for all these years!

Geraldine, Peter's 'sister', has found her real mother too, only a few miles away, but sadly she doesn't want to know her. Adrian, the other 'sister' has not done a search, as far as I know, and neither girls have chosen to marry.

Surprisingly, Kathleen remembered me, and spoke highly of me to Peter, so that is a relief! I must have done all the right things in her eyes!

He showed her the photographs that I took on the ship and in the park at Cape Town. Peter smiling as usual, and Kathleen and I both looking young and pretty in the sunshine!

I am surprised to find Kathleen is so much older than me. Peter is surprised that she is so small in real life. He also says she is very confused at times, which is natural after all these years, AND, she has never been able to read my story!

CHAPTER 21

Christmas 2,000.

Peter, Leanne, Madeline and Aiden, having now visited Kathleen several times in the nursing home, and been warmly accepted into the McGrath family, which is lovely, wish to move to Alice Springs.

There is more work for Peter looking after the Aborigines, and a good post for Leanne in the very busy hospital there. The schools are excellent for the children too.

The horses are sold, and the dogs are going with them, on the three day marathon drive. They assure me that they will stop off on the way!

Kathleen is now eighty, and has some of her immediate family nearby, to keep a watchful eye on her in the nursing home, so she should not miss them too much.

Peter and I have long chats on the telephone on a Sunday morning, and we also send e-mails to each other at regular intervals, which of course is cheaper and quicker.

I am still running my Domestic Cleaning Agency from home, Scott has his own successful Audio/Visual Company in Chiswick, and Gill and he have added a little granddaughter for me called Olivia.

Jean married Dr Pip Mounfield, a gynaecologist, and they live in Grimsby, S Humberside.

Sadly poor Graham died last year.

I now have a mobile phone, as have nearly the entire population of England!!

My Grandson, Max,
on his first day at school,5th September 2001

Gill

Scott

Olivia